W9-BGP-565

HISTORY OPENS WINDOWS

The VIKINGS

JANE SHUTER

Heinemann Library
Chicago, Illinois

© 2003 Reed Educational & Professional Publishing
Published by Heinemann Library,
an imprint of Reed Educational & Professional Publishing,
Chicago, Illinois
Customer Service 888-454-2279
Visit our website at www.heinemannlibrary.com

All rights reserved. No part of this publication may be reproduced or transmitted in any form or by any means, electronic or mechanical, including photocopying, recording, taping, or any information storage and retrieval system, without permission in writing from the publisher.

Designed by Roslyn Broder
Printed and Bound in the United States by Lake Book Manufacturing, Inc.

06 05 04 03 02
10 9 8 7 6 5 4 3 2 1

Library of Congress Cataloging-in-Publication Data
Shuter, Jane.
    The Vikings / Jane Shuter.
        v. cm. — (History opens windows)
    Includes bibliographical references and index.
    Contents: How were the Vikings ruled?—War—Religion—Ships—
    Expansion—Trade—Towns—Houses—Food and farming—Families—
    Clothes—Writing and storytelling—End of an empire.
    ISBN: 1-4034-0254-X (HC), 1-4034-0082-2 (Pbk.)
    1. Vikings—Juvenile literature. [1. Vikings.] I. Title. II. Series.
    DL65 .S54 2002
    948'.02—dc21

                                2002000805

Acknowledgments
The author and publishers are grateful to the following for permission to reproduce copyright material:
pp. 6, 8, 9, 13, 20, 22, 23, 26, 29 C. M. Dixon; pp. 10, 17 Werner Forman Archive, Statens Historiska Museum, Stockholm; p. 11 Werner Forman Archive; p. 12 Werner Forman Archive, Viking Ship Museum, Bygdoy; p. 15 Courtesy of Maine State Museum, Augusta, ME; p. 16 Statens Historiska Museum; p. 24 National Museum of Ireland; p. 25 York Archeological Trust; p. 28 Macduff Everton/Corbis; p. 30 Erich Lessing, Art Resource, NY

Illustrations: pp. 4, 14 Eileen Mueller Neill; p. 7 Juvenal "Marty" Martinez; pp. 19, 21, 27 John James
Cover photograph courtesy of C. M. Dixon

Every effort has been made to contact copyright holders of any material reproduced in this book.
Any omissions will be rectified in subsequent printings if notice is given to the publisher.

Some words are shown in bold, **like this.** You can find out what they mean by looking in the glossary.

A note about dates: in this book, dates are followed by the letters B.C.E. (Before the Common Era) or C.E. (Common Era). This is instead of using the older abbreviations B.C. and A.D. The date numbers are the same in both systems.

Contents

Introduction

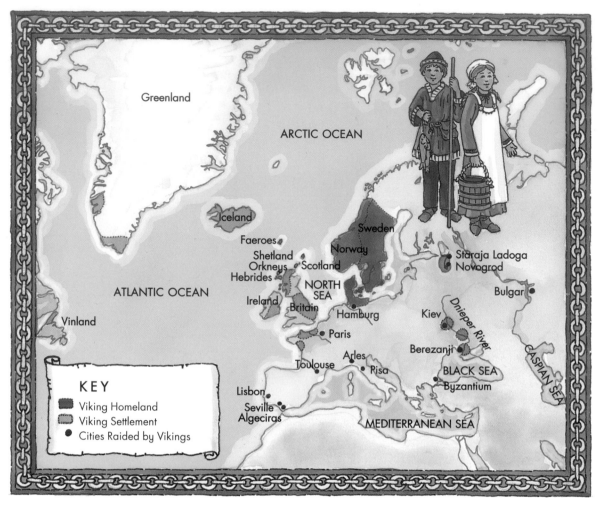

This map shows how far the Vikings traveled to raid and settle.

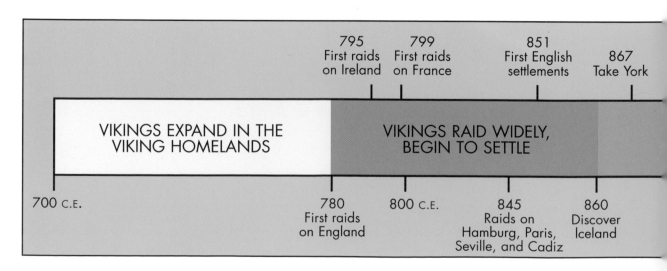

The Vikings lived in Norway, Denmark, and Sweden about 1,000 years ago. Starting in about 780 C.E., the Vikings **raided,** traded, and settled more and more of Europe, Iceland, Greenland, and North America. In their language, *viking* meant both "to travel" and "a pirate raid."

The Vikings were not a single group ruled by one king. Different groups of Vikings raided and traded in different places and saw themselves as different. But to the rest of the world, they were all Vikings. They spoke the same language, worshiped the same gods, and followed the same pattern of raiding and trading with countries before settling there. By about 1000 C.E. these groups had stopped "viking." They settled down and married local people. They were not Vikings anymore.

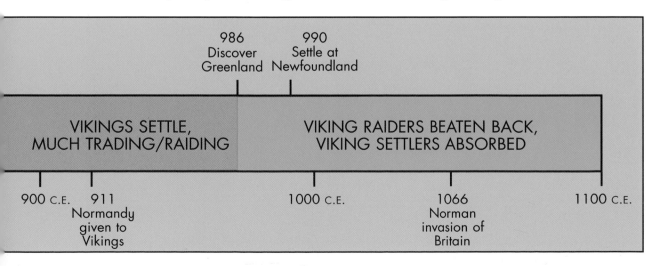

986 Discover Greenland

990 Settle at Newfoundland

VIKINGS SETTLE, MUCH TRADING/RAIDING

VIKING RAIDERS BEATEN BACK, VIKING SETTLERS ABSORBED

900 C.E.   911 Normandy given to Vikings   1000 C.E.   1066 Norman invasion of Britain   1100 C.E.

How Were the Vikings Ruled?

The Vikings did not have a single ruler. At first, the Vikings lived in villages made up of a few families. The leader of the village was the *jarl.* He did not make the decisions. He and all the other free men, or *karls,* of the village met regularly in a **Thing** to settle disputes, make laws, and punish crimes. Women and children could not join in a *Thing.* Neither could **slaves.**

As time passed, the Vikings joined up into bigger groups to be safer from attack. Soon there were towns and large settlements with many *jarls.* Sometimes several groups agreed to work together, also for safety. *Things* became bigger and the *jarls* did not always agree. So the Viking lands split up into several kingdoms. Each was run by a king chosen by the *jarls.*

These chess pieces were made in about 1150. The third figure from the left shows a Viking king.

Vikings

King

Jarls

Karls

Women
and
children

Slaves

Outlaws

7

War

War was part of the Viking way of life. Instead of fighting large-scale wars, different villages or kingdoms would fight. Viking groups traded with each other when they could, but if they needed food or land that another group had, they were prepared to fight to take it. The Vikings also seem to have expected to fight when they arrived somewhere new. Every man over the age of fifteen was supposed to have his own weapons and armor and be able to fight. The Vikings believed that a warrior who died in battle would go to a wonderful feasting hall in the afterlife called Valhalla.

These iron swords were found in the Viking city of Jorvik (now called York), in England. They are about 1,000 years old.

This stone was found on Lindisfarne, an island off the coast of England. It shows several warriors, usually said to be Vikings.

The Vikings fought with swords, axes, spears, and bows and arrows. They wore helmets and carried shields for protection. Some Vikings also wore chain mail. This was a **tunic** made from small links of metal joined together. Men from a village made their own fighting unit, which could have between 60 and 400 men. Because the groups were so small, they could recognize each other in battle. This was important, because many Viking groups had the same kind of armor and weapons. It could be hard to tell which side a person was on.

Religion

This tapestry shows three gods. Odin, the father of the gods and the god of wisdom, is carrying an axe. Thor, the god of war, is carrying a hammer. Frey, the god who made the crops grow, is carrying a stalk of corn.

At first, all Vikings were **pagans.** This means they believed in many different gods and goddesses that controlled different parts of everyday life. They told many stories about these gods and goddesses, who all lived together in big families—just like the Vikings. The gods and goddess argued, fought, and plotted against each other. They had to be kept happy, or they would keep the crops from growing, or make ships lose their way at sea. The Vikings also believed in other magical creatures such as trolls and **dwarfs.**

The Viking goldsmith who owned this mold made crosses for Christians and tiny charms that were supposed to be Thor's hammer for pagans.

As they traveled, the Vikings met more and more Christians. They began to change their religion to become Christians. Sometimes they did this because Christians would only trade with other Christians. Some Vikings became Christian because they were forced to when they lost a war. Many Vikings just added Christianity to their old beliefs, even though Christians were supposed to stop believing in the old gods. When a Viking king became Christian, he made all his followers Christian, too.

Ships

Ships were very important to the Vikings. They needed ships for exploring, **raiding,** trading, and carrying **settlers** to new lands. All Viking ships were built in the same way, by overlapping planks of wood. They had to be narrow, to sail up rivers. They all had square sails and a steering oar at the back. They were rowed with oars.

The smallest Viking ship, used by local traders, was 21 feet (6.5 meters) long and 4.5 feet (1.4 meters) wide. The largest to be discovered so far is 76 feet (23.3 meters) long and 17 feet (5.2 meters) wide.

This ship from Oseburg, Norway, was made in about 850 C.E. It was probably used for sailing on rivers or close to shore.

The Vikings were some of the first people to sail out of sight of land. They could do this by using the sun or stars to **navigate.** If they could not see the sky, they used a lodestone to navigate. This was a stone that was magnetic, so it swung towards the north, like a **compass.**

The Vikings traveled long distances in their biggest boats. Everyone had chests for their things, which they sat on to row. They slept on the deck and cooked food by lighting a fire in a box of sand.

Viking raiding ships often had fierce carvings at the front of the boat. They were meant to frighten the enemy as the ships came in to land.

Expansion

Starting in 860 C.E., the Vikings **raided** and **settled** in more and more places. They did this for several reasons. Traveling and raiding was part of the Viking way of life. Also, the further they traveled, the more places they found to trade with. An important reason for them to settle in other places was that the Viking homelands did not have much good farming land. As the Viking population grew, there were too many people to feed or find homes for. They needed to find new places to live.

This map shows Viking trade routes and the places they settled.

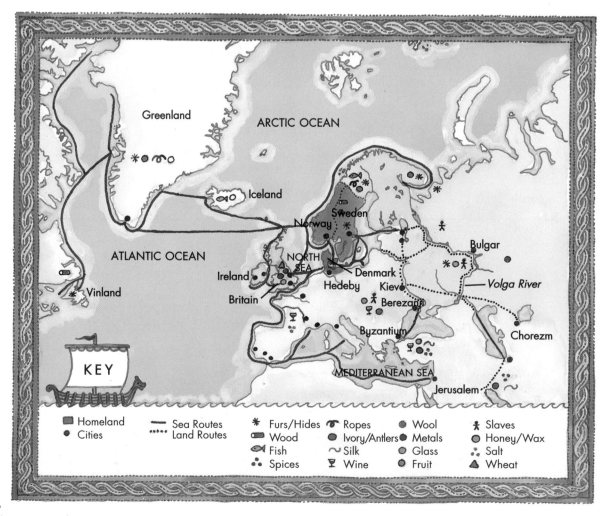

Greenland

ARCTIC OCEAN

Iceland

Sweden

Norway

NORTH SEA

ATLANTIC OCEAN

Ireland

Britain

Denmark

Hedeby

Vinland

Kiev

Bulgar

Volga River

Berezani

Byzantium

Chorezm

MEDITERRANEAN SEA

Jerusalem

KEY

🟥 Homeland	▬ Sea Routes	✳ Furs/Hides	🐚 Ropes	⬤ Wool	🏃 Slaves
● Cities	⋯ Land Routes	🟫 Wood	⬤ Ivory/Antlers	⬤ Metals	⬤ Honey/Wax
		🐟 Fish	～ Silk	⬤ Glass	⋮ Salt
		⋮ Spices	🍷 Wine	⬤ Fruit	🔺 Wheat

This Viking penny was found in Maine in 1957. Vikings probably did not live there, but other people living in Maine may have traded for it. The front and back of the penny are shown here.

The Vikings traveled all over the world. They behaved in a similar way wherever they went. If they found somewhere that had no people living there, they settled in it. If they found a place that had people living in it, they traded with them, took what they wanted without trading, or both.

After a while they began to spend the winters in these places, rather than going back to their homelands. Finally, they brought families out to settle.

Trade

We know which countries the Vikings traded with because **goods** from other countries have been found in Viking graves, towns, and settlements. The Vikings sailed to most of the places that they traded with. They went by sea all around Spain and into the Mediterranean Sea. They sailed up rivers, too, especially wide European rivers like the Volga and the Dnieper.

Viking traders often carried their own scales and weights. The trader would put metal coins in one dish and a weight in the other. If they balanced, he knew it was a fair trade.

Viking traders brought back silver from Russia, silks and spices from the Middle East, and wine from France. Coins from as far away as Arabia have been found in graves in the Orkney Islands, off Scotland.

The Vikings traded furs, fat, and **slaves** for the silks and spices they wanted. Viking towns such as Jorvik became trading points for merchants from Germany, Ireland, and the Viking homelands.

Viking traders brought back goods from all over the world. This beautiful gold necklace was found in Sweden, but it probably came from far away.

Towns

Most Vikings were farmers. They lived in small villages made up of large family groups. However, there were also many Viking craft workers and traders. These people needed to live and work in large settlements. Towns of different sizes sprang up in the places where the Vikings **settled.** Some of them were quite small. Others were larger—Jorvik had about 15,000 people living there at one time.

Viking towns were built on the coasts or on rivers wide enough for Viking ships to sail up. They had narrow streets. The houses and workshops were made from wood, with **thatched** roofs. Craft workers often lived in the same area, which made trading easier. People mainly traded from the street in front of their workshops. Animals were traded on certain days at certain places outside the town, where there was plenty of space.

This modern artist's view shows how the town of Jorvik would have looked from the air when it was at its biggest. It developed into the modern city of York, England.

old Roman wall

King's palace

Foss River

Ouse River

Houses

Wherever the Vikings settled, they built homes from the local materials. So in Iceland, which had very little stone or wood, they built long, low houses. The walls and roof were made from **turf.** In Shetland, there was enough stone to build the houses from stone. In Jorvik, houses were made from wood, with **thatched** roofs.

To iron clothes, Viking women used flat boards like this one, made from wood, bone, or stone. They ironed the clothes by smoothing them with a large, flat stone.

This illustration shows a Viking home in Jorvik, England.

Viking women wove their own cloth on looms like these.

The beaten earth **hearth** had stone walls surrounding it for safety. The fire was used for heat and cooking.

The toilet was outside the house, but not too far away.

The wide benches down either side of the house were used for sleeping or sitting.

Some homes had coops like this, to shut chickens in at night to keep them safe.

Food and Farming

Viking farmers grew different crops, depending on the weather in the places they were living. They all grew some kind of grain crop that could be used to make porridge, beer, and flour for bread. After the busy planting and **harvesting** time, farmers often went **raiding** to fill the gaps in their food supply.

Viking farmers kept chickens, geese, and ducks for eggs and meat. They kept cows, sheep, and goats for milk and meat, and pigs for meat. They used every part of the animals when they were killed. For example, skins were made into leather shoes or clothes, while bones were made into combs, pins, and blades for ice skates.

Vikings often made combs from the antlers of red deer. This comb has its own case.

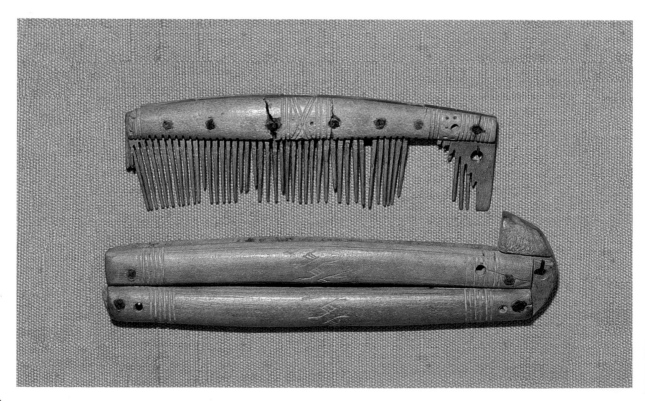

*This model of a Viking **hearth** shows cooking pots found in Iceland.*

The Vikings ate a lot of meat and fish, cooked over an open fire. They usually drank milk or beer. The two main meals of the day were eaten in the morning and in the early evening.

When two people got married, or if there was a successful raid or some other reason for celebrating, they held a feast. The feast could last for several days. There would be lots of speeches and storytelling, and whole animals would be **roasted** for eating. The men ate separately from the women and children—this kind of feast was for men only.

23

Families

Families were very important to the Vikings. They lived in large family groups that were more important than the smaller group of parents and their children. This was partly because many men spent part of the year away, **raiding,** trading, or exploring. Also, divorce was easy, so if a marriage was unhappy, people could part.

Most children lived at home until they were about ten. Then they went to live with another family, to learn a trade or how to keep house. Sometimes they had to move far away. If they lived close enough, they visited home when they could.

Families often passed the long wintertime by playing games. This board is for a battle game.

Boys were taught a trade and how to fight. They learned the trade of the person who brought them up. Sometimes this was the same trade as their father, but not always. Girls were taught how to run a home and bring up children. They had to learn how to cook, sew, and weave.

Women learned to run their husband's farm or business, too, so they could keep things going when the men were away raiding or exploring. However, they were expected to obey their husbands. They did not help to make decisions.

This scene is part of a tour of the re-created city of Jorvik. The man is using a foot-powered machine to make a wooden bowl.

Clothes

The Vikings wore warm, comfortable clothes. Most women spun, dyed, and wove the cloth for the family's clothes at home. Most cloth was spun from wool, although in some places **flax** and **linen** were used, too. All cloth was dyed with vegetable dyes.

Slaves made the cloth and the clothes for rich families. The very rich might buy silk cloth at markets. Shoes and boots were made of leather. Vikings who lived in cold places lined their boots and cloaks with sheepskin or fur.

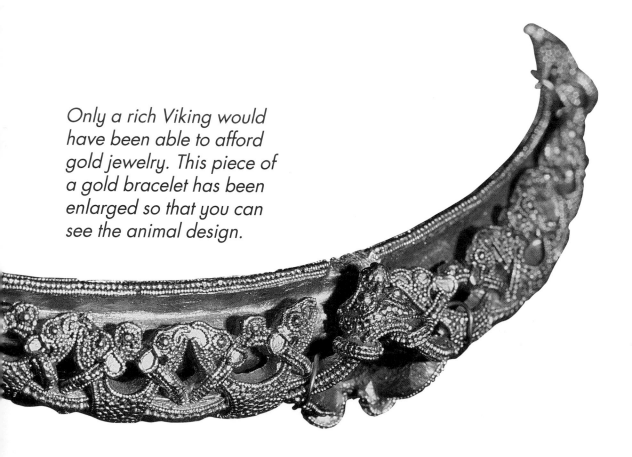

Only a rich Viking would have been able to afford gold jewelry. This piece of a gold bracelet has been enlarged so that you can see the animal design.

Women often wore an apron over their dresses, unless they were wealthy and not expected to do dirty work. Linen aprons were easier to wash and dry than heavy woolen dresses.

Children wore the same kind of clothes as adults.

Merchants who did a lot of trading often dressed well. They sometimes wore new kinds of clothes, brought back from their travels. This merchant is wearing baggy knee-length trousers, not the more typical long straight ones.

Kings and **jarls** wore the same kind of clothes as everyone else. But their clothes were made of more expensive materials, such as silk and fur.

Writing and Storytelling

The Vikings had a system of writing that used alphabet symbols called **runes.** The earliest runic alphabet had 26 symbols, but by 700 C.E. there were only sixteen.

Runes were used in carvings on stone markers and graves. They were sometimes used to keep records of trading.

The Vikings loved **sagas**— stories that often mixed up real history and made-up adventures. Sagas almost always had a hero who faced great dangers, dealt with the gods, but won in the end. Because runes took so long to carve, they were not used to write down the sagas or other stories.

This memorial stone has runes written all around the edge.

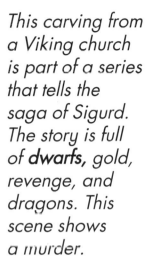
*This carving from a Viking church is part of a series that tells the saga of Sigurd. The story is full of **dwarfs,** gold, revenge, and dragons. This scene shows a murder.*

Instead, the Vikings had storytellers called *skalds* who told the sagas at feasts or on other special occasions. The sagas were very long, but they often rhymed. This made them easier to remember. A really good storyteller would change the sagas depending on the audience. If they were bored he would cut parts of them out, or he would string out the parts they were really enjoying.

Some storytellers also made up poetry. Poems were shorter than sagas and did not always tell a story. They also made up riddles, which the Vikings loved.

End of Empire

The Vikings were not suddenly beaten in battle. Those who had moved to live in other places **settled** down there. They often changed their ways and married into the local families. They became French or English or Russian. They no longer thought of themselves as Vikings. Those people who still lived in the Viking homelands **raided** less as Europe began to change and develop into more settled kingdoms. These kingdoms were not as easy to raid. So the Vikings settled for trading instead.

This part of the Bayeux Tapestry shows the Norman invasion of Britain in 1066. The Norman ships look a lot like Viking ships. This is because Vikings had settled Normandy.

Glossary

archaeologist person who studies people and objects from the past

artifact object made and used by people in the past

compass device with a magnetic needle that always points north

dwarf in Viking stories, dwarfs were small human-like creatures

flax plant that can be made into cloth

goods things made or grown to trade or sell

harvest season when crops are gathered; or, to gather a crop

hearth area in front of a fireplace

jarl Viking leader who ranked below the king

linen smooth, strong cloth made from the flax plant

navigate to find the right direction during a journey

pagan person who believes in many gods and goddesses

raid to attack a place, take what you want, and then leave

roast to cook for a long time in an oven

rune symbol in Viking writing

saga Viking story containing history and fables

settler someone who goes to a new land to live and work

slave someone who belongs to someone else and is forced to work without pay

thatched having a roof made out of grass or other plants

Thing group of Vikings who met to make decisions

tunic garment shaped like a knee-length T-shirt

turf soil held together by the roots of grass and other plants

More Books to Read

Chrisp, Peter. *Vikings.* Chicago: World Book, Incorporated, 1998.

Hopkins, Andrea. *Viking Families and Farms.* New York: PowerKids Press, 2002.

Ross, Stewart. *Read About Vikings.* Brookfield, Conn.: Copper Beech Books, 2000.

Index